ANTIQUE PLAYING CARDS

A PICTORIAL TREASURY

Henry René D'Allemagne

Selected and Arranged by
CAROL BELANGER GRAFTON

DOVER PUBLICATIONS, INC.
Mineola, New York

Copyright

Copyright © 1996 by Dover Publications, Inc.
All rights reserved under Pan American and International Copyright Conventions.

Published in Canada by General Publishing Company, Ltd., 30 Lesmill Road, Don Mills, Toronto, Ontario.
Published in the United Kingdom by Constable and Company, Ltd., 3 The Lanchesters, 162–164 Fulham Palace Road, London W6 9ER.

Bibliographical Note

This Dover edition, first published in 1996, is a selection of illustrations from *Les Cartes à Jouer du XIVe au XXe Siècle*, published by Librairie Hachette et Cie, Paris, in 1906. A new Publisher's Note and captions based on the French text have been written specially for this edition.

Library of Congress Cataloging-in-Publication Data

Allemagne, Henry René d', 1863–1950.
 [Cartes à jouer du XIVe au XXe siècle. Selections. English]
 Antique playing cards : a pictorial treasury / Henry René d'Allemagne ; selected and arranged by Carol Belanger Grafton.
  p.   cm.
 ISBN 0-486-29265-7 (pbk.)
 1. Playing cards—Collectibles—Pictorial works.   I. Grafton, Carol Belanger.   II. Title.
GV1235.A55213   1996   96-25991
                                                    CIP

Manufactured in the United States of America
Dover Publications, Inc., 31 East 2nd Street, Mineola, N.Y. 11501

PUBLISHER'S NOTE

ALTHOUGH THE origin of playing cards is a topic on which few scholars agree, there is a general consensus that they were first used in China at some time between the seventh and tenth centuries. The means by which they reached Europe is also far from clear, and the first reference to them appears to have been made in Italy in 1299.

There were two distinct types of decks of cards: those modeled on the cards from the East, which were similar to the divisions used today—suits, numbered cards and face cards—and the tarot deck, consisting of 22 cards, each depicting a particular virtue or vice. Although both types were used for games of pleasure, the tarot were used (as they are today) for purposes of fortune-telling. Eventually the two were combined to form a deck of 78 cards that is still in use in some parts of Europe.

For recreation and gambling, however, it was the four-suit deck that gained favor. In English, the suits are spade, heart, diamond and club; in French, *pique* (pike), *cœur* (heart), *carreau* (square) and *trèfle* (trefoil); in German, *Grün* (leaf), *Herz* (heart), *Schelle* (bell) and *Eichel* (acorn); in Spanish, *espada* (sword), *copa* (cup), *oro* (gold) and *basto* (rod); in Italian, *spada* (sword), *coppa* (cup), *denaro* (money) and *bastone* (rod).

At first, cards had to be created by hand, limiting their use to the affluent. But the development of wood engraving allowed them to be produced more economically. In fact, there is evidence that woodblock printing may have first been used to produce playing cards. Because of its opacity, pasteboard was used for cards.

From time to time novelty decks have been popular, either for educational or satirical purposes. Many are represented in this volume and feature historical and allegorical figures, gods, goddesses, astrological figures, animals and heraldic devices. Since the thrust of the book from which they are reproduced is primarily French, it is possible to trace the monarchy, the Revolution, the First Empire, the Restoration and the Second Empire on various decks of cards.

The designs of the cards range from the boldly stylized to delicately illustrative. In many instances the style is deliberately archaic; the design commonly in use today depicts the picture cards in the garb worn during the reigns of Henry VII and Henry VIII.

Double-headed fantasy cards, published by Leclaire, Paris, 1881.

Tarot deck, alleged to have belonged to Charles VI, fifteenth century.
TOP, LEFT TO RIGHT: The Fool, the Knave, the Emperor.
BOTTOM, LEFT TO RIGHT: The Pope, the Lovers, Fortune.

Cards with animal pips (suit of birds), engraved by the Master E. S., 1466.

Round deck of cards engraved in Cologne, ca. 1477.
TOP ROW, LEFT TO RIGHT: King of Parrots; Queen of Parrots; Higher Jack of Parrots.
SECOND ROW, LEFT TO RIGHT: Lower Jack of Parrots; Ace of Parrots; King of Pinks.
THIRD ROW, LEFT TO RIGHT: King of Hares, Queen of Hares, Higher Jack of Hares.
FOURTH ROW, LEFT TO RIGHT: Lower Jack of Hares, Ace of Hares, King of Columbines.

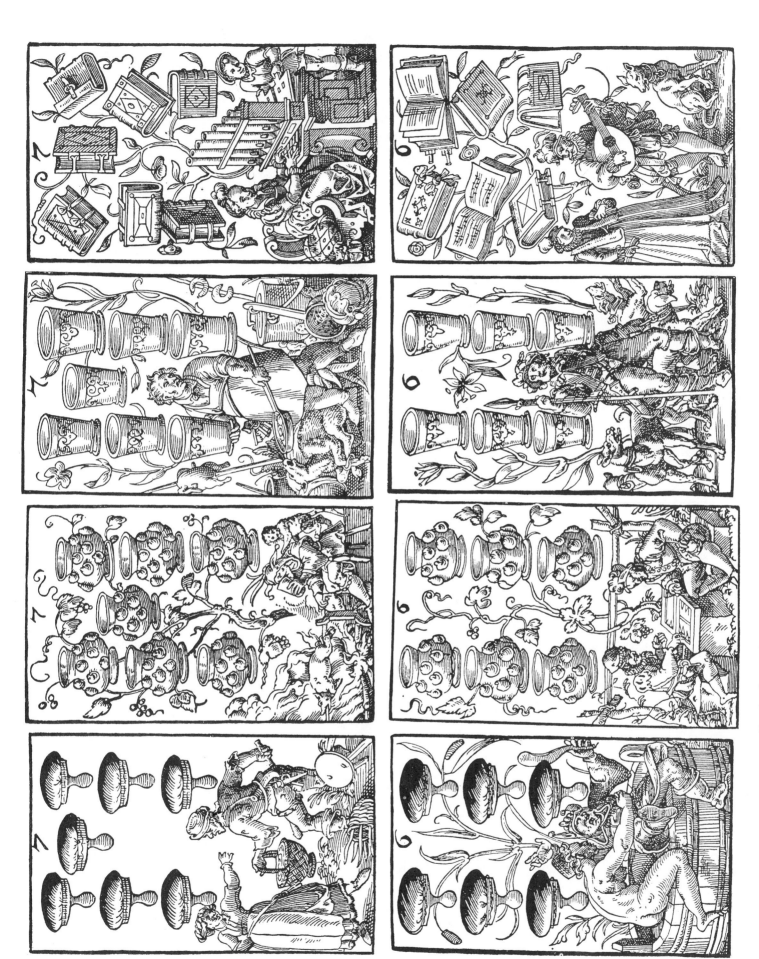

Deck of moralizing cards, wood engraving by Jost Amman, sixteenth century.

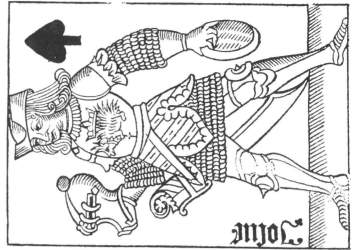
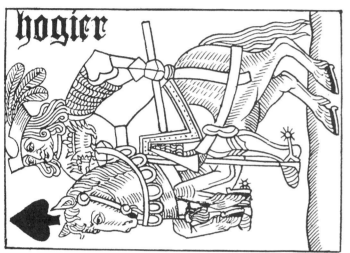

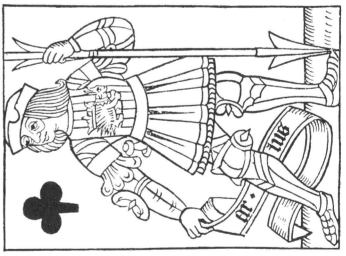

French cards with the crest of Louis XII, published by Master Artus, ca. 1500.

Parisian deck of cards published by Jean Trioullier, 1681–1703.

VIVE LE ·ROY ·

IEME · LA · MOVR ·

· ET · LA · COVR

Cards from a Parisian deck, second half of the seventeenth century.

Picture cards in the Provence style, published by Antoine Bonnier,
Montpellier, 1703.

Plate of jacks in the Auvergne pattern, end of the seventeenth century.

Wrappers for six decks of cards.
TOP: From the cardmaker Pierre Moussin, Nantes, 1760.
BOTTOM: From the cardmaker Claude-François Prost, Besançon, 1755.

Picture cards in the Dauphiné style, published by Jehan Genevoy,
Lyons, 1591–97.

Satirical German cards (jacks) engraved in 1545.

Cards with pips of flowers, fruits, birds and animals. Middle of the
seventeenth century.

Cards with symbols, of Parisian manufacture, published in the middle of the seventeenth century.

G. DE·BOVRDAVX

G.ENE·DE·BOVRDAVX

GENE·DE·BOVRDAV

G.·DE·BOVRDAVX

GVIENNE&BEAR·

GVIENNE&BEAR·

GVIENNE&BEA

GVIE&BEAR

GVIE&BEAR

16   Picture cards from Guyenne, first half of the eighteenth century.

ROY DE DENIER

ROY DE BASTONS

ROY · DESPEE

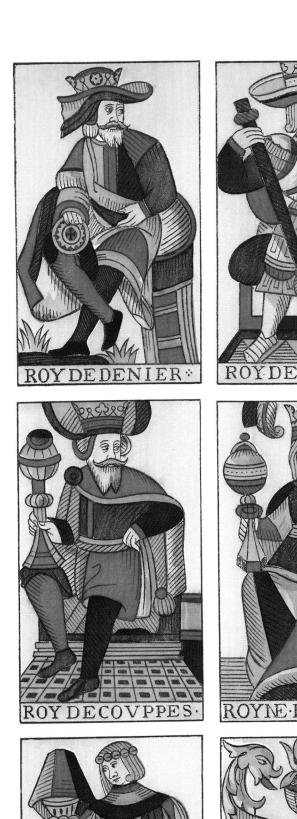

ROY DE COVPPES ·

ROYNE · DE COVPES

CHEVALIER DE COVPES

VALET DE COVPES

I · NOBLET · AV FAV
BOVR · ST GERMAIN

Cards with Spanish suits, Paris, mid-eighteenth century.

Tarot cards supposedly owned by Charles VI.
TOP, LEFT: the Emperor; TOP, RIGHT: Strength.
BOTTOM, LEFT: Temperance. BOTTOM, MIDDLE: the Jack of Swords.
BOTTOM, RIGHT: Justice.

Deck of cards of the Revolutionary period, 1792.

Première Carte

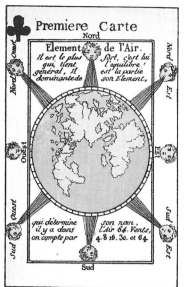

Première Carte
Nord

Element de l'Air.

Il est le plus / qui tient / général, il / dominante est. *fort, c'est lui / l'équilibre / est la partie / son Element.*

Nord — Est — Est
Ouest — Est
Ouest — Sud Est
Sud

qui détermine / il y a dans / on compte par *son nom, / l'Air 64 Vents, / 4.8.16.32. et 64.*

Première Carte

Elément de la Terre.

La Terre est portée par l'Eau et soutenue par l'Air, il est compact, il est la partie dominante ce qui lui donne son nom, la Terre a environ neuf mille lieues de circuit, on la divise en quatre Parties, savoir l'Europe, l'Asie, l'Afrique et l'Amérique, elle renferme dans son Globe 1,019,700,000 d'habitans.

Le Génie de la liberté trouve ou déterre — *Fabrication des Salpêtres*

dans le Sein de la Terre

Première Carte

Element du Feu.

Il est léger et le plus vif, lorsqu'il domine il consume et décompose tout, rien ne peut exister sans lui. Les Elémens sont inséparables et ne peuvent exister l'un sans l'autre.

Le Feu est d'un grand secours pour — *le Feu Républicain est plus fort*

la liberté, mais

Première Carte

Elément de l'Eau.

Il porte la Terre, le soleil le pompe et le rend, il est dans la même quantité depuis le commencement des Elémens ou de la Création du Monde, il est sept fois plus grand et plus étendu que la Terre.

l'Eau prête sa surface — *d'un Pole à l'autre*

pour porter la liberté

Seconde Carte

Seconde Carte

LE PRINTEMPS

Germinal / Floréal / Prairial

Je suis la Loi expression solennelle — *de tous les Citoyens*

de la volonté

Seconde Carte

L'ÉTÉ.

Messidor / Thermidor / Fructidor

Je suis la force et l'Espérance — *et la terreur des Tyrans*

des Républicains,

Seconde Carte

L'AUTOMNE

Vendémiau / Brumaire / Frimaire

Si nous voulons conserver la — *Armés dans tous les tems*

République, soyons

Seconde Carte

L'HIVER.

Nivos / Pluvios / Ventos
Fait par Bezu à Egalité sur Marne ci-devant Château Thierry

Malgré les rigueurs des Saisons, je resterai — *ma Mèche que la liberté n'ait affranchie l'Univers.*

à mon poste et n'éteindrai

Troisième Carte

Troisième Carte.

LA PROVIDENCE.

Le Sage reconnoît sa Justice éternelle, — *au murmure contre elle.*

et l'insensé la prie

Troisième Carte

LA LOI.

Force a la LOI
La Droits de Loi ...

La Loi dans tout Etat doit être — *quels qu'ils soient sont égaux devant elle*

universelle; les Mortels

Troisième Carte

LA LIBERTÉ

Indivisibilité

Vous avez la liberté, — *de la conserver.*

soyez digne

Troisième Carte

L'EGALITÉ

les Hommes sont Egaux

Les Mortels sont égaux ce n'est — *seule Vertu qui fait la différence.*

point la naissance, mais la

Deck of cards of the Revolutionary period, Château-Thierry, 1790–92.

Deck of cards designed by Houbigant, ca. 1818.

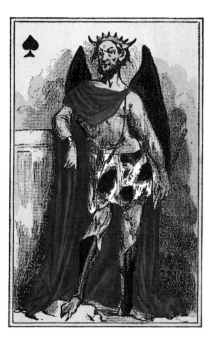

Fanciful deck of cards, era of Louis-Philippe, attributed to Nanteuil.

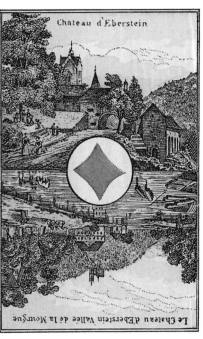
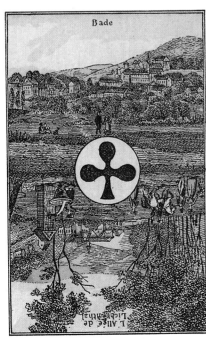

German double-headed picture cards, ca. 1860.

ROI DÉCHU.

Partant pour la Syrie..............

LA SAINTE ALLIANCE.

Ils viennent jusques dans vos bras.
Egorger vos fils, vos compagnes.......

CARLISTE.

............Hélas! Hélas!
Le bien - aimé ne revient pas.

PRESSE PÉRIODIQUE.

Vive la typographie
Pour servir la liberté!.........

GÉNÉRALE, TOCSIN.

Mais au premier son du Tambour,
Il sacrifie
A sa Patrie
Son bien, sa vie
Et son Amour,

LES TROIS POUVOIRS.

Fin de l'air du Dieu des bonnes gens.
Cette union constitutionnelle,
De qui pour tous naît la sécurité,
O genre humain, tu ne trouveras qu'en elle
La paix, la liberté!

LA VICTOIRE.

La Victoire en chantant nous ouvre
la Barrière.......

DOCTRINAIRE.

Ne dérangez pas le monde.
Laissez chacun comme il est.........

Deck of cards of the barricades, 1832.

French tarot cards executed in the seventeenth century by an unknown Parisian card manufacturer.

LE CHÊNE ET LE ROSEAU.

L'arbre tient bon, le roseau plie.

LE COQ ET LE RENARD

Car c'est double plaisir de tromper le trompeur.

LE RENARD ET LES POULETS D'INDE

*Le trop d'attention qu'on a pour le danger
Fait le plus souvent qu'on y tombe.*

LE LIEVRE ET LA PERDRIX

*Il ne se faut jamais moquer des miserables
Car qui peut s'assurer d'être toujours heureux.*

LA LAITIERE
ET LE POT AU LAIT

*Quel esprit ne bat la campagne ?
Qui ne fait châteaux en Espagne ?*

LES DEUX PIGEONS.

*Amans, heureux amans, voulez vous voyager
Que ce soit aux rives prochaines.*

LE POT DE TERRE
ET LE POT DE FER

*Ne nous associons qu'avec nos égaux,
Ou bien il nous faudra craindre
Le destin d'un de ces pots.*

LES GRENOUILLES
QUI DEMANDENT UN ROI

*Donnez nous, dit ce peuple, un roi qui se remue
Le monarque des dieux leur envoie une grue.*

LES VOLEURS ET L'ANE

*Un quart voleur survient qui les accorde net
En se saisissant du baudet.*

Instructive cards, depicting the fables of La Fontaine, Paris, ca. 1820.

M^d DE PANIERS

Marchand de paniers, sébiles de bois, sébiles de bois.

M^{de} DE CHIFFONS

Avez vous des chiffons à vendre voilà la march^{de} de chiffons

GAGNE PETIT

A repasser ciseaux, couteaux

M^{de} DE POIS

Pois ramés; pois écossés.

M^{de} DE CERNEAUX

Mes beaux cerneaux.

M^d DE CHAINES

La sûreté des montres.

M^d DE LEGUMES

Des choux, des poireaux, des carottes; navets, navets.

M^{de} D'HUITRES

Voilà l'écaillère, à la barque, à la barque!

CARRELEUR DE SOULIERS

Carreleur de souliers.

Deck of cards of the street cries of Paris, 1830–40.

Picture cards of the kings and queens from "Deck of Cards for a Joke," each
representing a paper published during the Second Restoration.

Cards from a fantasy deck, published by Jean Rolichon, Lyons, 1660–74.

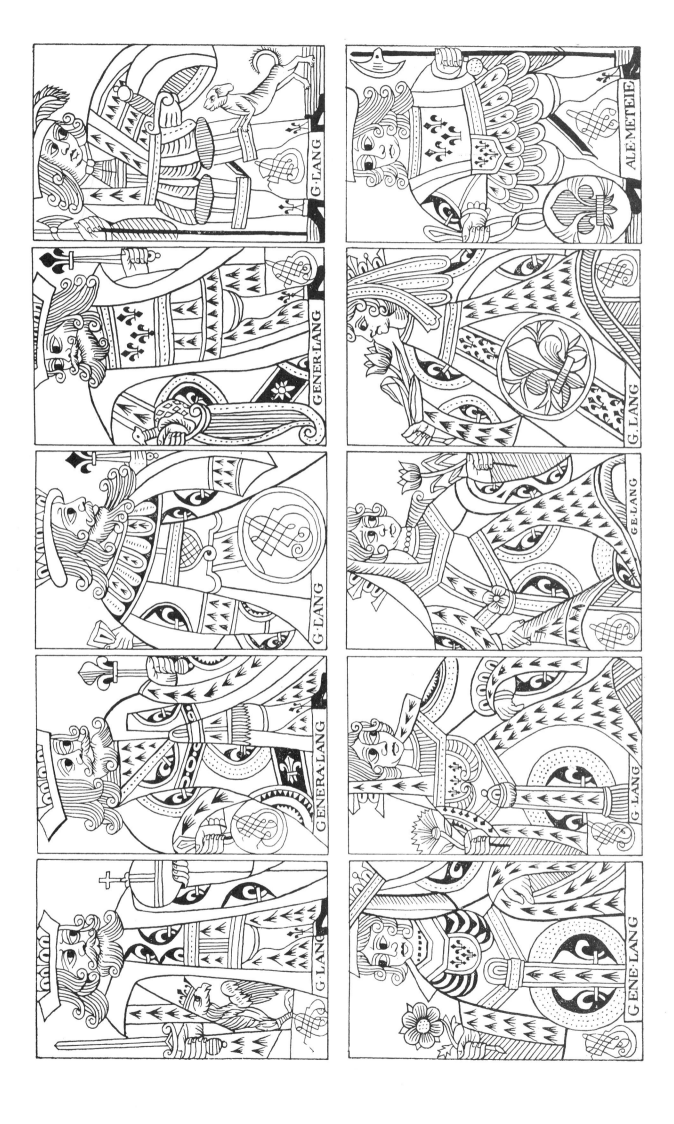

Picture cards in the Parisian style, ca. 1716–19.

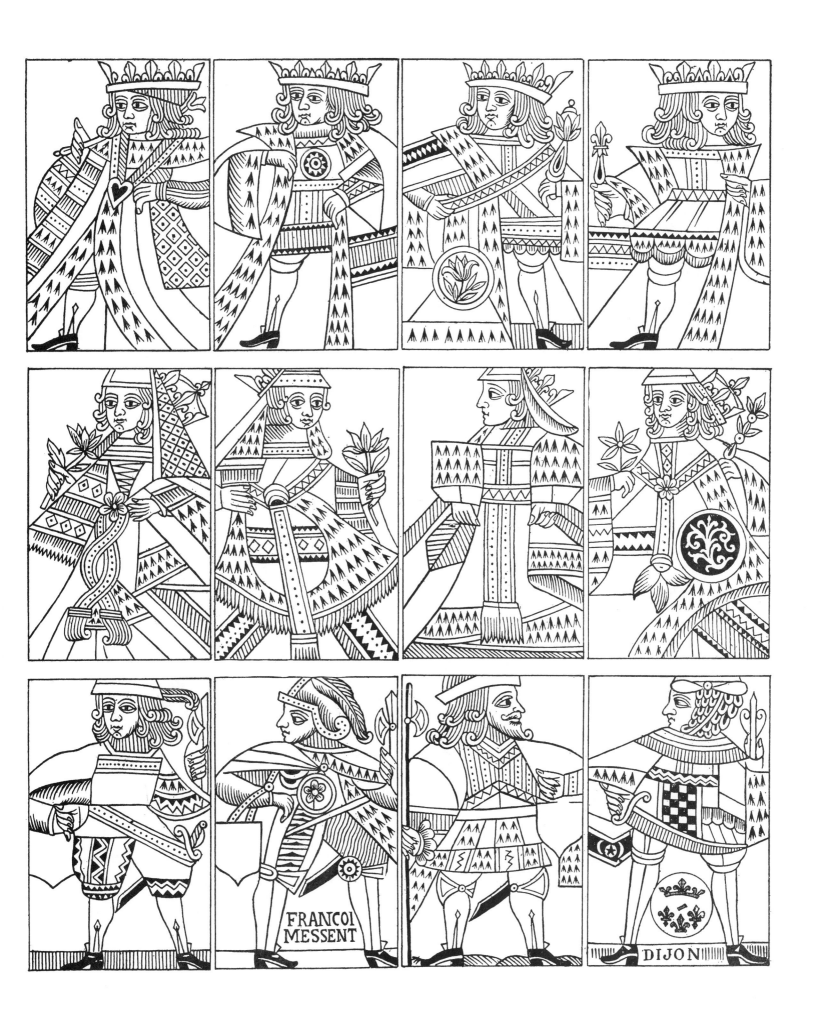

Picture cards in the Burgundian style, ca. 1752.

Picture cards in the Auvergne style, ca. 1701–02.

Picture cards in the Guyenne style, ca. 1746.

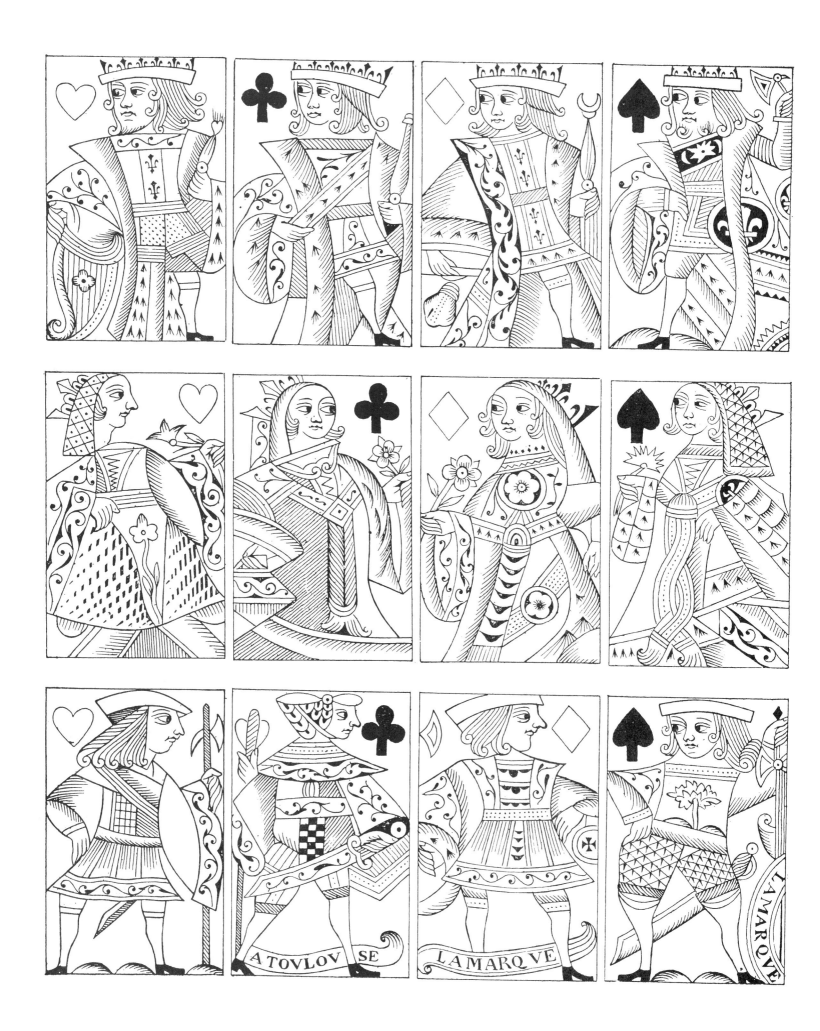

Picture cards in the Languedoc style, published by Lamarque, ca. 1720.

Cards from a Revolutionary deck, published by Pinaut, Paris.

Picture cards in the Parisian style turned into a Revolutionary pack by
Delâtre, Paris.

Imperial deck engraved by Andrieu, after sketches by David, 1808–10.

Picture cards in the official style, 1816.

HENRI IV. | Francois I.ᵉʳ | Sainct Loys | KAROLUS MAGNUS

JEANNE D'Albret. | Marguerite de Valois. | Blanche de Castille. | HILDEGARDE

SULLY. | Bayard | Le Connétable. | ROLAND

Cards from the recasting of the deck created by Houbigant,
published by Mme. Dambrin, ca. 1818.

40   Fantasy deck from the Second Empire.

Republican deck created by Bertrand, ca. 1872, published by Maison
Leclaire, Paris.

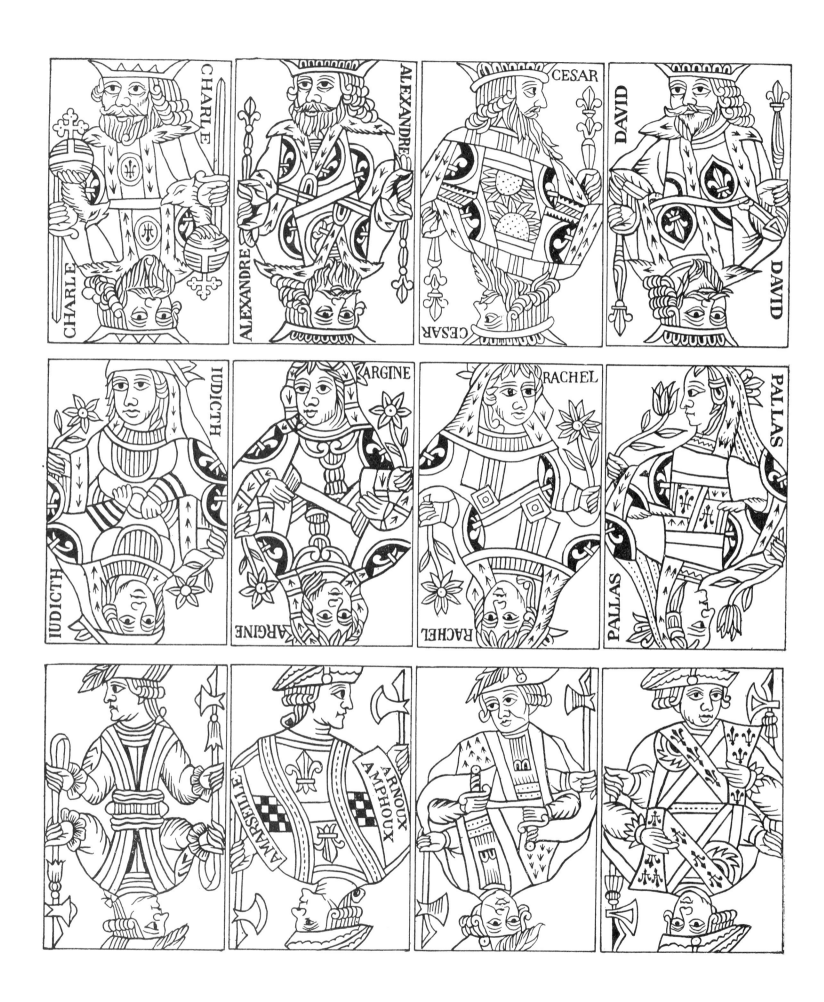

Double-headed picture cards, published by Maison Arnoux et Amphoux,
Marseilles, 1806.

IEVNESSE   RICHESSE

DIEU

DAVID · DE · SA · HARPE · LOVE · DIEU · DE · TOVT · SON · COEVR

CARTES · TRES · FINES · FAITES · PAR · ANTO.E

A · LA · FLEVRS · DES · CARte

CARTE · TRES · FINE · AV · ARME · DE
MONSIEVR · LE · COMTE · DESTIN · FAITE
A · LA · MODE · DE · PARIS · PAR · GVILLAVME ·
ROVGET · MAITTRE · CARTIER · DE · PARIS · ET
DE · THIERS · DEMEVRANT · EN · RVE · DES
PETTIS · GRAS · A · CLERMONT · PAR · PRIVILEGE ·

TOP: Wrapper for a deck of cards, probably from Normandy,
eighteenth century. BOTTOM: Wrapper for six decks of cards by
Guillaume Rouget, eighteenth century.

Political deck, published by Maison Grimaud, 1872.

Double-headed picture cards for the Swiss market, nineteenth century.

ROY DEPEE

CHEVALIER DESPEE

ROY DE DENIERS

VALET DE BATON

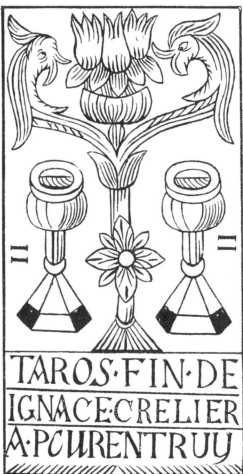

TAROS·FIN·DE
IGNACE·CRELIER
A·PCURENTRUY

VALET DE COUPES

Tarot cards from a deck published by Ignace Crelier, Porentruy, 1781–1803.

XII

·LE·PENDV·

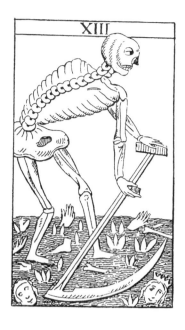

XIII

XIIII

·TENPERANCE·

XV

·LE·DIABLE·

XVI

LA·MAISON·DIEU

XVII

·LESTOILLE·

XVIII

LALVNE·

XVIIII

·LE·SOLEIL·

XX

·LE·IVGEMENT·

XXI

·LE·MONDE·

·LE·MAT·

Trumps from a tarot deck, eighteenth century.

47

Swiss deck, seventeenth century.

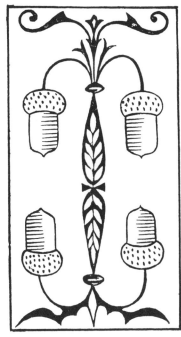

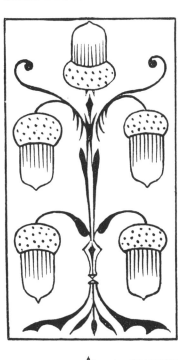

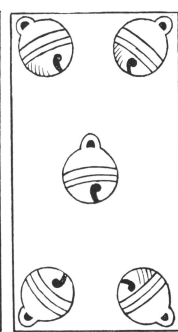

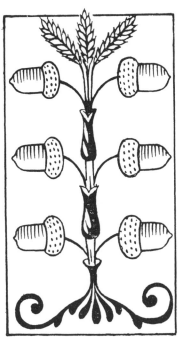

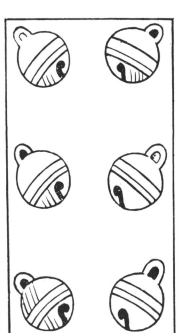

Number cards from a Swiss deck, seventeenth century.

Educational deck by Murner, sixteenth century.

King ♣

Q. Elizabeth prepares a strong
Fleet, L.ᵈ Howard, L.ᵈ Seymor, S.ʳ
Francis Drake Commanders.

Queen ♣

The Pope gives a Million of
Gold to help the Spaniard.

Knave ♣

Cardinal Allen renews the Bull
of Pope Pius to absolve ƴ Queen's
Subjects from their Allegiance

I ♣

The Pope and Traiterous
English fugitives consult
the Conquest of England

II ♣

King of Spain consults the
enldrging his Empire by the
Conquest of England.

III ♣

Don Bassano Commander in
cheife ordered to begin the
Invasion with great Ships.

IV ♣

Don Alancorn Vicar-General
for the Inquisition with a
traine of 100 Monkes & Fryers

V ♣

Five Regiments of old Spanish
Soldiers.

VI ♣

124 Noblemen and others of
the greatest houses of Spain
Voluntiers.

Deck dating from the English Revolution of 1688, depicting events relating
to the Spanish Armada of 1588.

Novelty deck, published by Terquem et May, Metz, 1819.

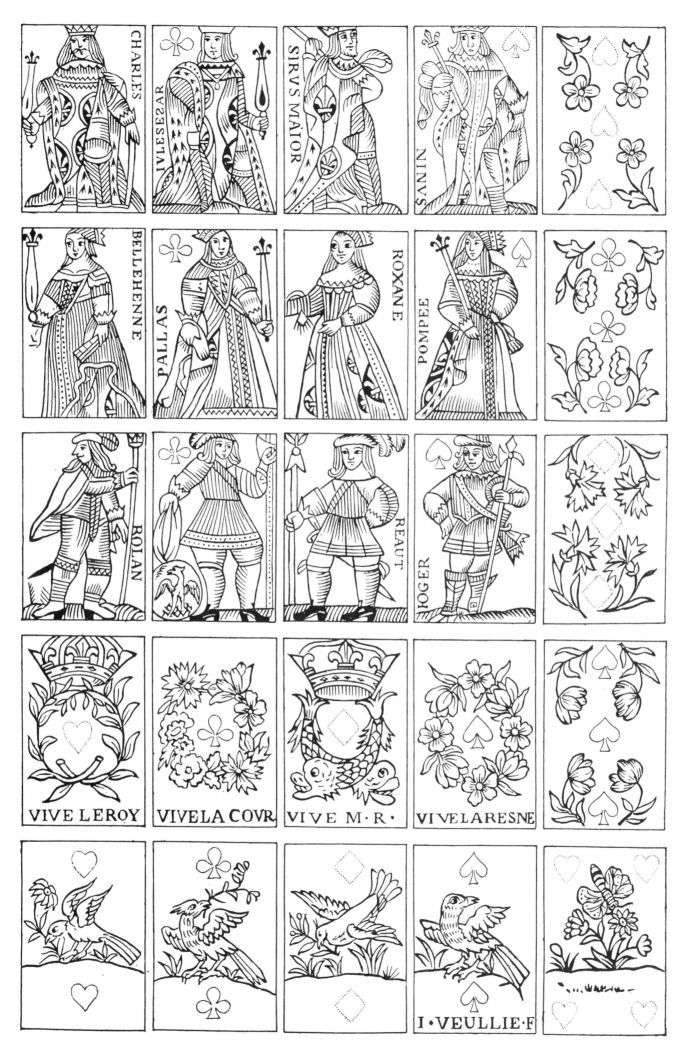

Children's picture cards in the seventeenth-century Parisian style,
published by J. Veuillié at the end of the eighteenth century.

Picture cards in the Parisian style, published by François Ratoin, Rouen, 1720.

TOP: Card wrapper of Hugues Lyet, Nantes, 1755–58.
BOTTOM: Wrapper for six decks of cards, Louis Chaffard, Béziers, 1748.

Fantasy cards engraved by Virgil Solis, sixteenth century.

Fantasy deck, published in Paris, 1835.

Astronomical cards intended for fortune-telling.

Cards with Spanish suits with the mark of Francisco Tourcaty,
published by Claude Langlois, Paris, 1758.

Grotesque deck, Paris, 1820.

VOULEZ · VOUS
FAIRE·LE·VOYA
GE DE · CITHERE

PAS · DU · TOUT

AIMEZ · VOUS · LE
DON
SOURIRE·DE·CUPI

SUR·CE LA
CONSULTEZ
MES · YEUX

INFINIMENT
SUR LE · · GAZON

JE VEUX · VOUS
FAIRE · UNE
CONFIDENCE

ETES · VOUS · REBELLE
DANS · LES · TETES
A · TETES

QUEL · QUE · FOIS

SI JE VOUS LE DISOIS
EN DOUTERIES VOUS

ETES · VOUS
AMOUREUSE

PUIS JE · COMPTER
SUR · VOUS

CELA · NE · SE · DIT
PAS

Deck of cards of questions and answers, Revolutionary era.

le Curé.

Sœur de la Mariée.

Importun

8.

M^{de} à la Toilette.

Importun

4.

la Prude.

Importun

12.

le Rival ridicule.

Importun

13.

le Clarinette

Importun

2.

la Bouquetière.

Importun

16.

le Suisse.

Deck of cards of "The Dowry or the Game of the Bride," (1820–30).

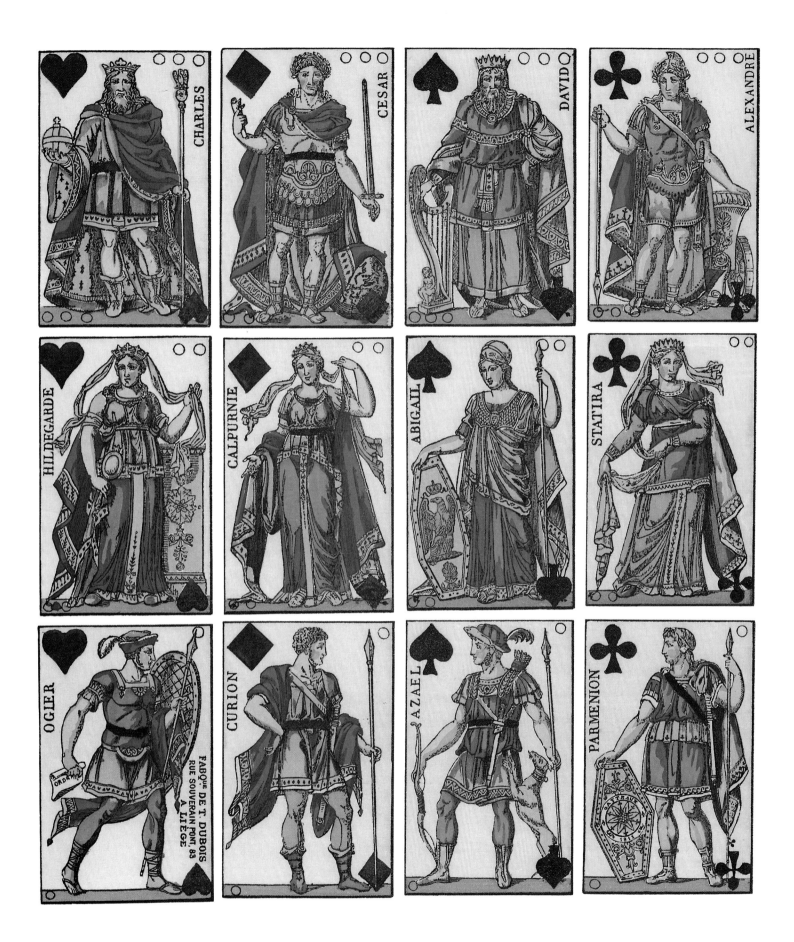

Deck of cards, Liège, 1811.

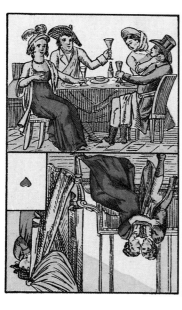   

Deck of cards for fortune-telling, executed during the Restoration.

Deck of cards, published by Robert Passerel, Paris, 1622.

RÉ PUBLICAIN

RÉ PUBLICAIN

RÉ PUBLICAIN

RÉ PUBLICAIN

JARDINNIER

JB DEBEI NE A REIMS

VENDANGEUR

MOISSONNEUR

BUCHERON

Jacks from Revolutionary decks of cards, Paris and Reims.

Cards from an *alluette* deck, Nantes, beginning of the nineteenth century.

Fantasy cards, beginning of the seventeenth century.

Deck of cards of the Revolutionary period, Paris, 1792.

GRAND HONNEUR.   RENTIER.   HOMME DE COMMERCE.   HOMME DE ROBE

TENDRESSE.   AMOUR D'ARGENT.   MÉCHANTE FEMME.   FEMME VEUVE.

GÉNÉROSITÉ.   FLATTEUR   UN MILITAIRE.   MESSAGER

"The Little Sorcerer," a fortune-telling game, beginning of the
nineteenth century.

Deck of cards of the rulers of Europe, end of the Second Empire.

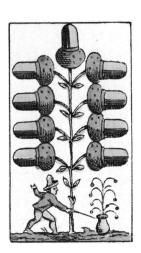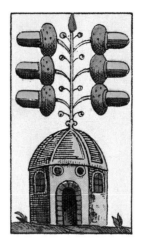

Children's game with German suits, featuring the depiction of a balloon, Munich, eighteenth century.

Duplication of Jaume and Dugourc's deck, Nantes, late eighteenth century.

Picture cards from Guyenne, late seventeenth century to ca. 1740.

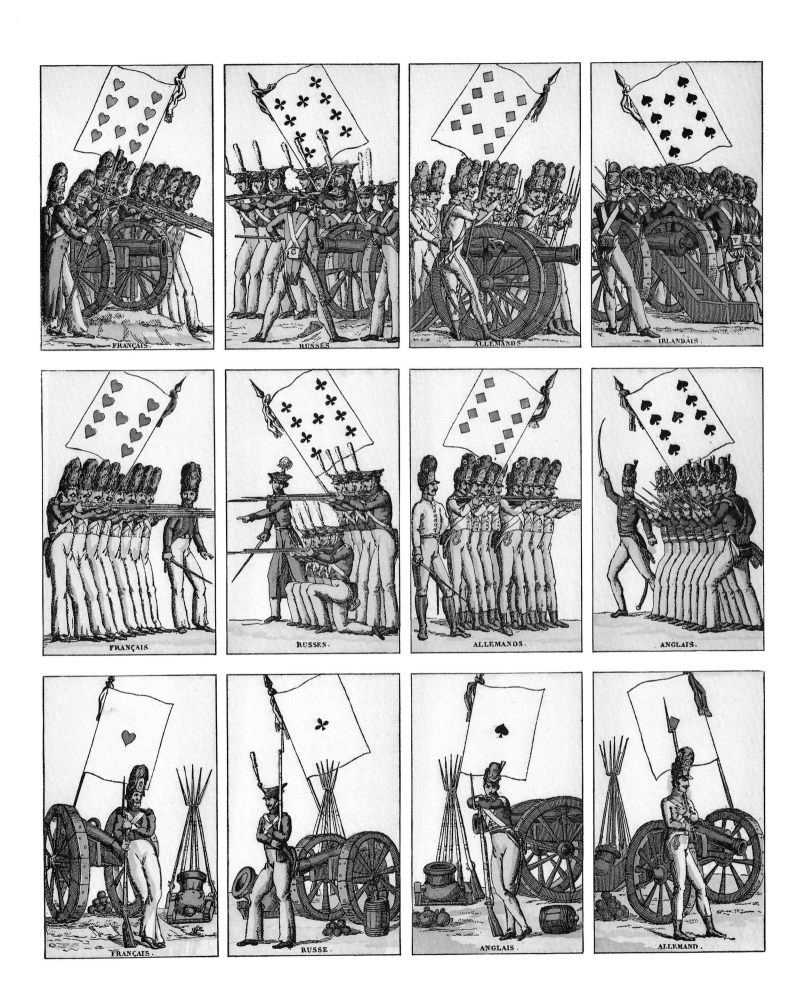

Number cards from the game of the flags, after a deck published during the Restoration.

Double-faced English picture cards, London, end of the nineteenth century.

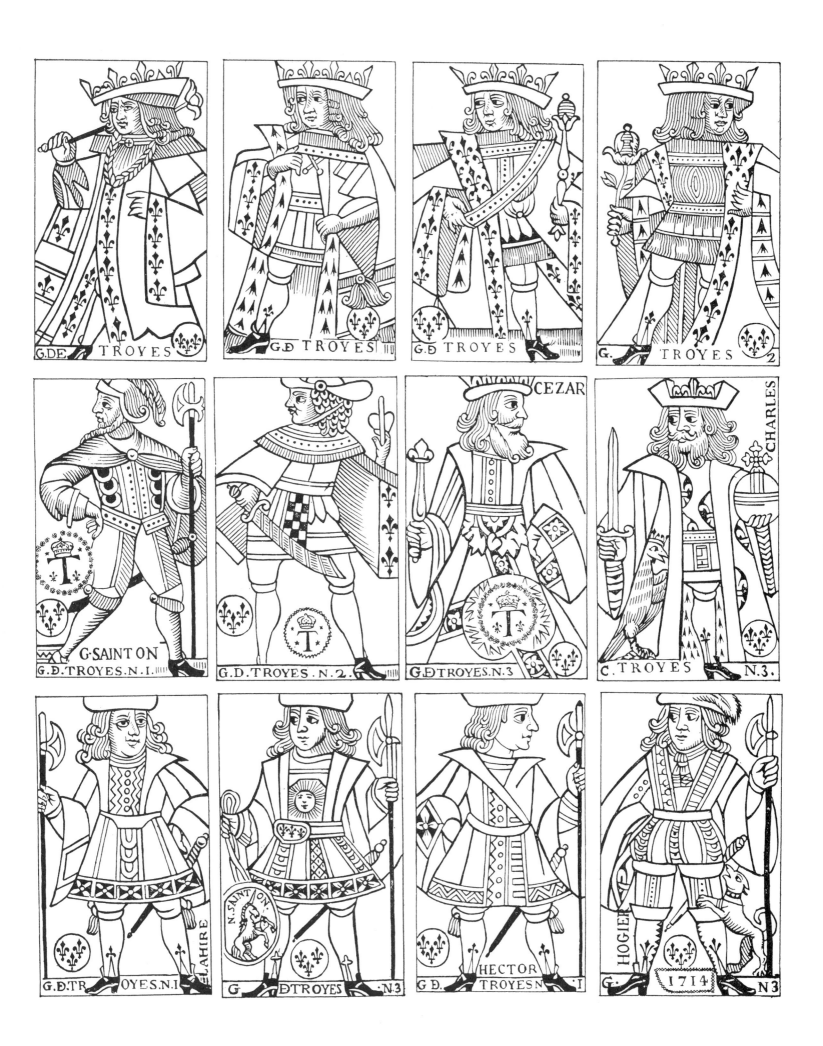

Picture cards in the styles of Burgundy and Paris, published in Troyes, 1701–04.

French cards drawn and painted by hand, end of the fifteenth century.

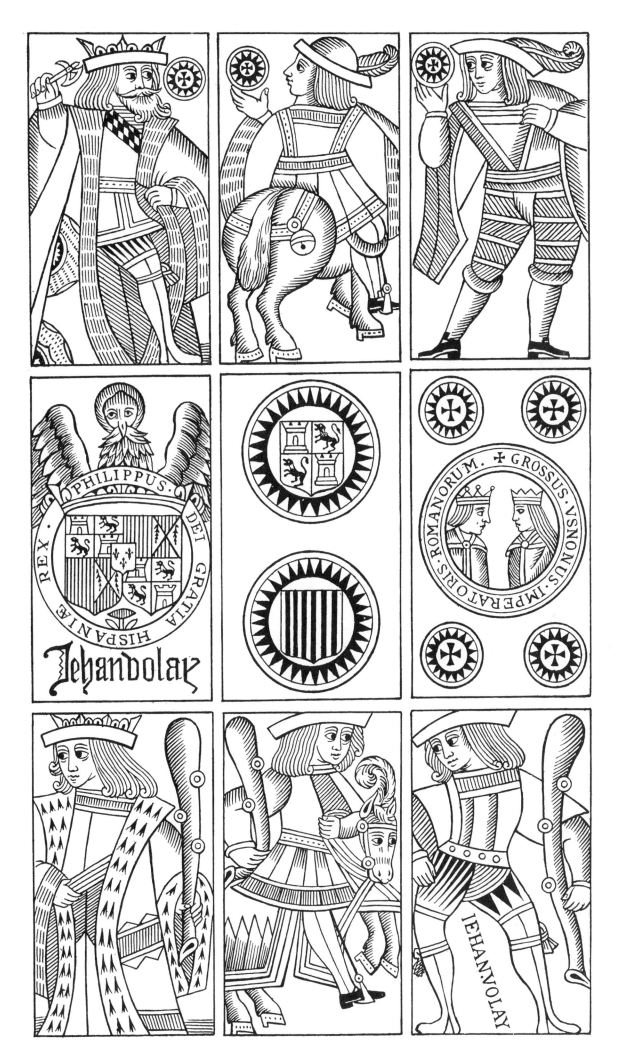

Cards with Spanish suits published in Thiers, under the mark of
Jehan Volay, ca. 1700.

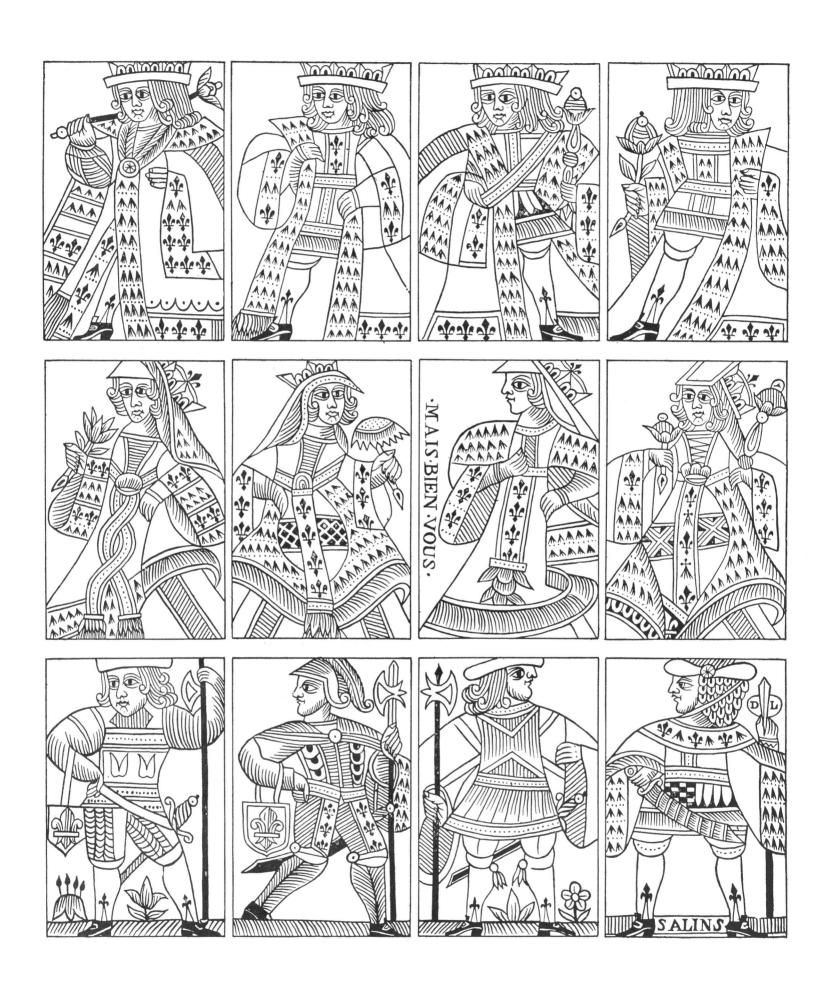

The cards bear the inscriptions: ·MAIS·BIEN·VOUS· and SALINS.

Picture cards in the Burgundian style, 1748.

Revolutionary deck, published by Barbarin, Lyons, 1793.

Cards with Spanish suits, published by Jehan Volay, Thiers,
eighteenth century.

Card wrappers. TOP, LEFT: By Nicholas le Roy, Paris, 1719.
TOP, RIGHT: By Estienne le Sieur, Troyes, 1722–61.
BOTTOM, LEFT: By Nicolas Housset, Paris, 1734–46.
BOTTOM, RIGHT: By Pierre Archange, eighteenth century.

Cards with Spanish suits, published by Francisco Tourcaty, Marseilles, 1701–36.

Pirated picture cards in the Provence style, eighteenth century.

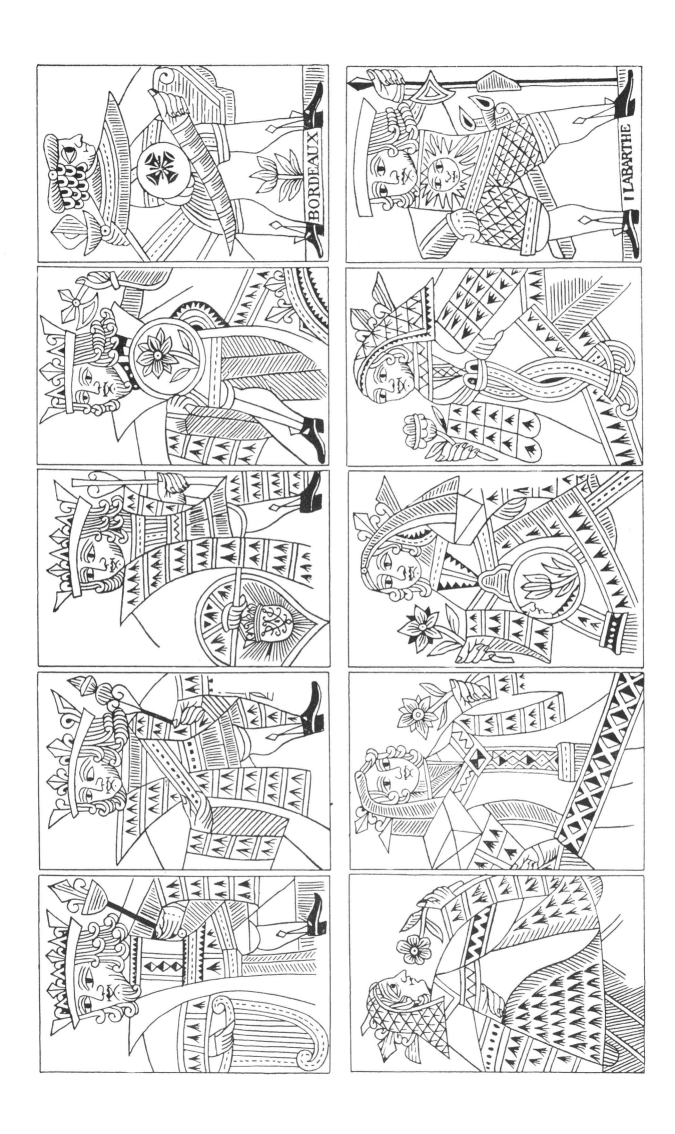

Picture cards in the Guyenne style, 1773.

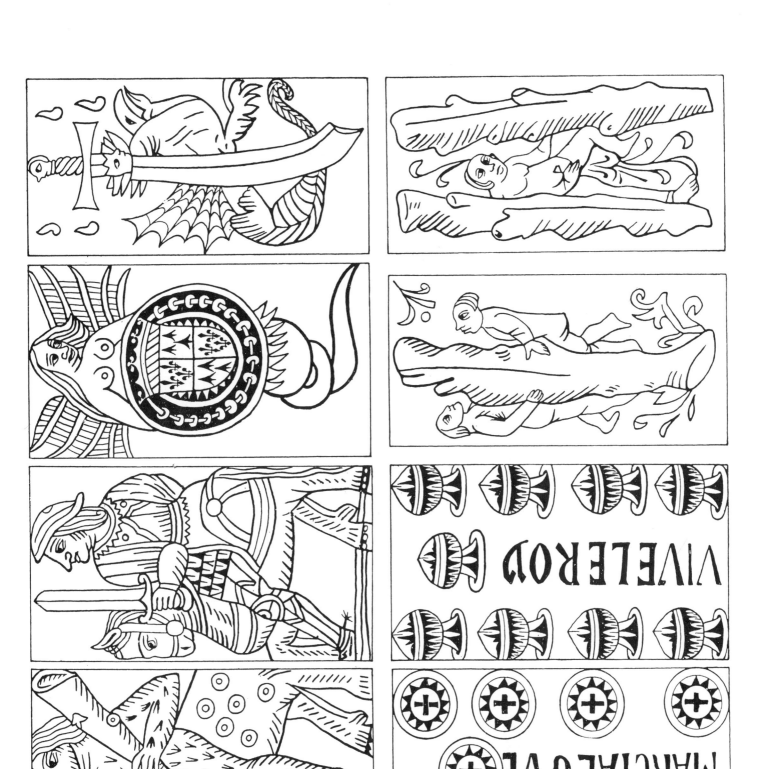

Cards with Spanish suits, published by Martial Gué, Limoges, 1538.

Revolutionary picture cards in the Limoges style, published by
Jacques Bessé, Angoulême.

Deck of royal emblematic figures, created in honor of the accession of
Louis XVIII, published by Bayard, Paris, 1816.

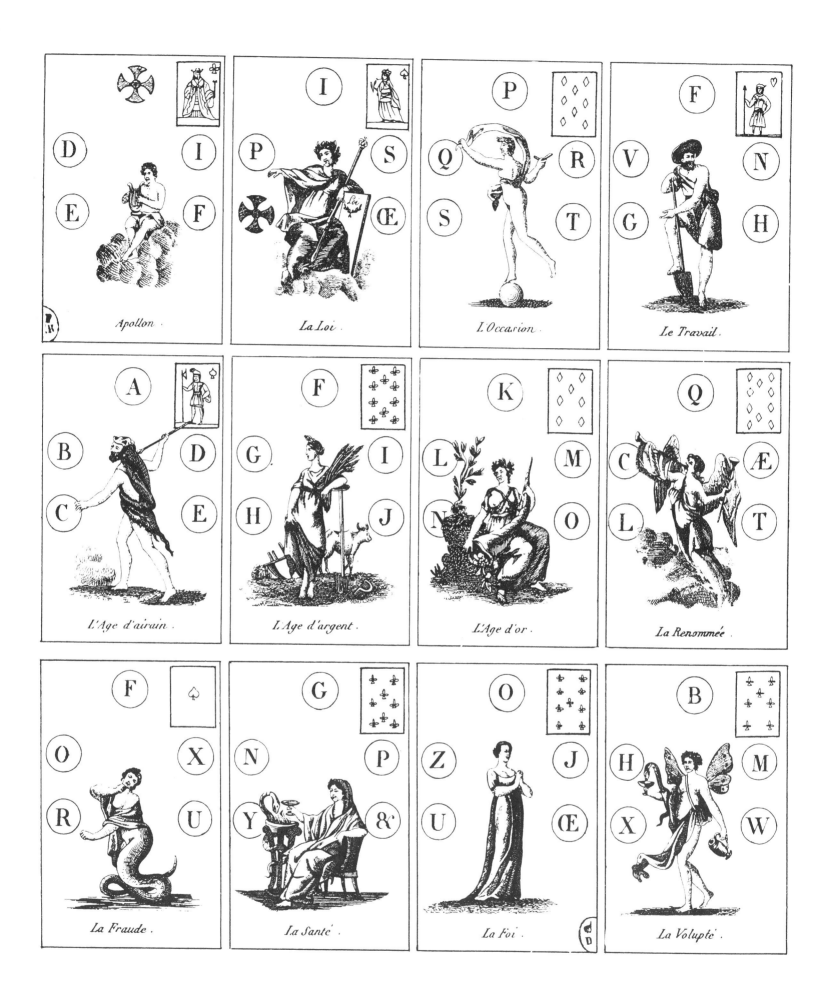

Apollon.

La Loi.

L'Occasion.

Le Travail.

L'Age d'airain.

L'Age d'argent.

L'Age d'or.

La Renommée.

La Fraude.

La Santé.

La Foi.

La Volupté.

Fortune-telling deck, engraved by Bouchard, Paris, during the Restoration.

TOP: Cards with Spanish suits, published by Guymier, Paris, 1574–94.
MIDDLE: Cards for the game of the Royal Comet.
BOTTOM, LEFT TO RIGHT: Four of Swords and Four of Rods as used in Italian
decks from the fifteenth to twentieth centuries; Ace of Rods and
Ace of Swords from a tarot deck published by Fautrier, Marseilles, 1753–93.